INTENTIONAL SHIFT FROM CRISIS TO CONTROL

INTENTIONAL SHIFT FROM CRISIS TO CONTROL

Robyn T. Jones

Lift & Shift
PUBLISHING

© 2025 Robyn T. Jones
All rights reserved.

No part of this publication may be reproduced, distributed, or transmitted in any form or by any means, including photocopying, recording, or other electronic or mechanical methods, without the prior written permission of the author, except in the case of brief quotations embodied in critical reviews and certain other noncommercial uses permitted by copyright law.

For permission requests, please contact:
Robyn T. Jones
Innovative Leadership Solutions, LLC
www.robyntjones.com

Published by Lift & Shift Publishing, an imprint of Innovative Leadership Solutions, LLC

ISBN: 979-8-9987974-0-8
Printed in the United States of America.

Cover design by DMP Designs

First Edition, 2025

DEDICATION

To the Lord —
Thank You for being my strength when I was weak, my peace in the chaos, and the rock that held me steady through every storm.
You helped me grasp the power of intentionality as it relates to every aspect of my life, especially my journey to health.
This book is a testimony of Your grace, faithfulness, and the life-changing power of surrender and making an impact.

And to my beloved mother, Jessie M. Hardaway —
You were my first anchor and the truest example of servant leadership.
Through your grace, strength, wisdom, and unwavering faith, you taught me to live boldly, love deeply, and lead with purpose.
Your life was — and still is — a living blueprint for the woman I strive to be.
Though you are no longer physically here, everything you poured into me continues to light my path.

FOREWORD

It is said that life's greatest lessons are often learned through our greatest struggles. I have been blessed with a front row seat in watching Robyn walk through her journey of navigating crisis, embracing intentional living, and stepping fully into her purpose. She has not only lived the words you are about to read —she has embodied them with grace, determination, and an unwavering commitment to growth.

Intentional Shift: From Crisis to Control is not just a book; it's an invitation to transform your life from the inside out. Robyn's heart for helping others shines through every page. What you hold in your hands is not just theory, it is lived experience. It is hope wrapped in action and a guide with real tools and encouragement to shift you beyond a life of survival into a life of clarity, peace, and purpose.

I couldn't be more proud of Robyn for sharing her heart and journey so openly. My hope is that you find yourself not only inspired but empowered to take intentional steps in your own life. So, open your heart and mind and remember, no matter where you find yourself today, a SHIFT IS POSSIBLE!

Contrell Jones
Proud Husband and Greatest Supporter
#TeamJones4Life!

Table of Contents

Introduction	1
Why the Shift Matters	7
The Cost of Crisis Mode	11
The Shift from Crisis to Control	27
Intentional Shifting: Four "A" Steps	
Awareness: Recognizing the Patterns	
Acceptance: Owning Your Power	
Alignment: Setting Your Intentions	
Action: Creating the Change You Seek	
Life Anchors: Faith, Family, and Friends	39
Anchoring Your Shift: Reflections & Journaling	49
The Lift & Shift™ Challenge	57
The Shift Starts Now	61
Recommended Reading	65
Next Steps for Your Intentional Shift	67
Acknowledgements	69

INTRODUCTION

Life can feel like a never-ending cycle of stress, demands, and obligations. For years, I operated in what I now call "crisis mode"—reacting to everything around me instead of intentionally shaping my life to live it out at its fullest. For over 14 years, my life had seemingly been plagued with one health crisis after the next. I just accepted it all until one day, **I made an intentional shift in my mind, body and spirit**. I decided it was time to take control and be intentional in taking my life back. As a woman of faith, I have heard many preachers say, "God will do His part, but you must do yours." I finally decided it was time to do my part so I could live a healthy and fulfilling life.

I was never a sickly person other than the regular winter cold and flu. However, in 2010, at the age of 40, my life took a turn I never saw coming. From April to August 2010, I found myself back and forth from one medical specialist to another. I didn't know exactly what was wrong, but I knew whatever was happening internally wasn't normal. After having a spinal tap to rule out Multiple Sclerosis (MS), I was finally given a diagnosis of Systemic Lupus Erythematosus (SLE). The day-to-day exhaustion, sensitivity to sunlight, chronic body aches, and the need to sleep in the middle of the day turned life as I once knew it upside down.

After several changes to my medicine cocktail, my rheumatologist suggested I undergo infusions. I didn't think twice. If anything could help me have a better quality of life, I was on board and willing to try. Lupus held its grip on me for 10 years until I was faced with another crisis.

As I walked in my office in February 2021, I met my office manager clinching my chest as I felt as if I was having a heart attack. Needless to say, I was rushed to the ER and was admitted for five days. I was seen by cardiologists, gastroenterologists, and pulmonologists – nothing was found to be wrong. However, as my food trays kept coming, I noticed they had me on a diabetic diet. I was well aware that I was pre-diabetic, but during this hospital stay, I found out that I was now fully diabetic.

In 2002, my late mother, Jessie Hardaway, died at age 67 from complications to diabetes as well as both her parents. Thus, the news of being a diabetic took me to a dark place and the crisis mode went into overdrive. The one thing I always told the Lord was that I could deal with anything, but **I never wanted to live with diabetes**.

> **The news of being a diabetic took me to a dark place and the crisis mode went into overdrive.**

But there I was, a diabetic, crying, angry and in total denial. A month later, the chest pain started again, and this time I was encouraged to see an orthopedic doctor who specialized in the spine. And wouldn't you know it, the chest pains were deriving from issues with my cervical spine.

Intentional Shift: From Crisis to Control

While I continued to wish the diabetes away, not changing anything in my lifestyle and barely taking the prescribed diabetes medication, the cervical spine issue became worse. However, while going through all the medical clearances needed to have spinal surgery, my PCP called with more heart wrenching news. They could not clear me to have the surgery because my calcium levels were highly elevated. I was referred to an endocrinologist, who had me undergo a myriad of tests. And wouldn't you know it – I needed parathyroid surgery before I could undergo spinal surgery.

On December 30, 2022, I underwent parathyroid surgery. What should have been a three-to-four-week recovery ended up being three months. The overwhelm of it all had me mentally spiraling and I felt no one understood the angst I was experiencing internally. My life felt totally out of control. After fully recovering from parathyroid surgery, I finally underwent ACDF surgery in September 2023. Because **I was living in crisis mode**, I did not realize that my diabetes was out of control.

On April 27, 2024, I faced a serious health crisis where I stood at the threshold between what was…and what could have been the end of my life. This health crisis forced me to seriously confront my diabetes diagnosis and all the ways in which I was living in a state of crisis. It finally clicked and I realized something had to change. I couldn't keep living on autopilot, hoping things would get better. I had to make an *intentional decision* to shift and do life differently. This book is an invitation for you to do the same—to shift from living a life of crisis to control and step into a life of intention, purpose and balance.

What You'll Gain from This Book

This is not just another book filled with inspirational words—it is a guide to action. By the time you finish reading, you will have a clear roadmap to:

- Identify where you are currently living in crisis mode.
- Recognize patterns that keep you stuck in reactive living.
- Learn practical tools to shift your mindset and habits.
- Establish a strong foundation for sustainable, intentional living.
- Gain confidence in making decisions that align with your purpose.

It finally clicked and I realized something had to change. I had to make an *intentional decision* to shift and do life differently.

Intentional Shift: From Crisis to Control

This book is for you if you have ever felt:

- Overwhelmed by daily demands and responsibilities.
- Trapped in unhealthy cycles but unsure of how to break free.
- Disconnected from your true passions and purpose.
- Ready to take control of your life but don't know where to start.

If any of these resonate with you, then you are in the right place.

How to Get the Most Out of This Book

To fully embrace intentional living, I encourage you to engage with this book actively rather than just reading passively. Here's how you can make the most of this experience:

Pause & Reflect – Each section contains thought-provoking questions and journal prompts. Take time to write your responses on the lines provided or in a separate journal or notebook.
Take Action – Small, intentional changes lead to lasting transformation. As you read, identify at least one actionable step from each chapter and apply it to your daily life.
Stay Committed – Shifting from crisis to control doesn't happen overnight. Give yourself grace but stay committed to your journey. Revisit sections of this book as needed for

reinforcement and encouragement.
Connect & Grow – You don't have to navigate this journey alone. Join my community of like-minded women who are also on the path to intentional living. Together, we can support, encourage, and uplift one another.

> **Your transformation begins with one decision: to show up for yourself, fully and intentionally.**

Your transformation begins with one decision: to show up for yourself, fully and intentionally. Let this book be your companion, your mirror, and your launchpad into a life that finally feels like yours.

WHY THIS SHIFT MATTERS

"Life is always moving, changing, shifting into its next shape. The movement is natural. It is how we evolve. Let the shifts happen. Take responsibility for yourself each step of the way. Trust the new shape and form of your world"

~ Melody Beattie

Many people move through life feeling like they are simply surviving, running from one obligation to the next without ever pausing to ask: **Is this the life I truly want?**

When we operate from a place of exhaustion and reaction, we lose sight of what's possible. The beauty of life lies in reclaiming our power, making intentional choices, and designing a life that aligns with our values and aspirations. Living in crisis mode doesn't just take a toll on your mental and physical health—it impacts your relationships, career, and overall sense of purpose. My personal journey led me to this realization.

> **Living in crisis mode doesn't just take a toll on your mental and physical health—it impacts your relationships, career, and overall sense of purpose.**

Before my health scare, I thought I was in control, but in reality, I was simply managing chaos. I was constantly putting out fires, meeting everyone else's needs while ignoring my own. It took a life-threatening wake-up call for me to understand that if I didn't take control of my life, and more specifically my health, I would never live life to its fullest. And that's what I want for you—to experience the freedom and fulfillment that comes when you shift from merely surviving to intentionally thriving.

> I thought I was in control, but in reality, I was simply managing chaos.

The shift matters because your life matters.

We often normalize survival mode so deeply that it becomes our lifestyle. We settle for "fine," tolerate disconnection, and quiet the whispers of our dreams because we believe this is all life has to offer. But here's the truth: *you were not created to merely cope—you were created to contribute, to connect, to live on purpose.*

When we choose to shift, we reclaim our personal power. We begin to understand that peace is not something to chase—it's something to protect and cultivate from within. Crisis no longer defines us. Instead, clarity becomes our compass.

Intentional Shift: From Crisis to Control

Shifting allows you to:

- Reclaim your **personal power** and stop outsourcing your peace to circumstances.
- Discover your **true values**, rather than living by the demands of others.
- Restore **joy** in everyday moments instead of waiting for a someday that never comes.
- Reconnect to your **why**, your purpose, and your calling.

The shift is not only about leaving behind the chaos; it's about moving toward clarity. It's about showing up to your life—fully present, fully awake, fully committed to your growth. And it begins the moment you decide to stop waiting for the world around you to change, and instead, take responsibility for your internal transformation.

> **The shift is not only about leaving behind the chaos; it's about moving toward clarity.**

When You Shift, Everything Changes.

You begin to speak differently—more intentionally, more truthfully. You begin to act differently—with courage, with clarity, and with conviction. You begin to prioritize differently—choosing alignment over approval, peace over performance.

This shift matters because it is the foundation for everything else you desire. It's what gives you the energy to pour into your family without emptying yourself. It's what helps you set boundaries that protect your peace without guilt. It's what awakens you to the truth that you *get to live on purpose, not by pressure.*

As you lean into this shift, you will notice that your dreams will no longer feel like distant hopes but reachable realities. Your relationships will deepen, your confidence will grow, and your capacity to experience genuine joy will expand. The life you envision isn't as far away as it seems; it is waiting on the other side of your decision to be intentional.

So yes, the shift matters. Because you matter. And the life that's waiting for you on the other side of chaos? It's worth everything it takes to get there.

Let this be your reminder: the shift isn't just possible. It's powerful. And it starts with you.

THE COST OF CRISIS MODE

Many of us don't realize we're living in crisis mode because it has become our day-to-day normal. We wake up exhausted, push through the day, take care of everyone else, and collapse at night—only to repeat the cycle tomorrow. This way of living leads to burnout, strained relationships, poor health, and a loss of purpose. For some, it is all we know because we have normalized this chaotic way of thinking, living, and doing.

> Many of us don't realize we're living in crisis mode because it has become our day-to-day normal.

What is Crisis Mode?

Crisis mode is a state of constant reactivity where we operate on autopilot, responding to urgent demands rather than intentionally shaping our lives. It's the feeling of always being behind, never catching up, and constantly firefighting through the day. This is an exhausting way to live, yet many people don't realize they are in crisis mode until they hit a breaking

> "Don't wait until you're in crisis to come up with a crisis plan."
> -Phil McGraw

point. As Dr. Phil McGraw wisely said, "Don't wait until you're in a crisis to come up with a crisis plan."

Imagine driving a car with the gas pedal pressed all the way down but with no clear destination. Eventually, you'll run out of fuel, break down, or crash. That's what living in crisis mode feels like—running at full speed without a sense of direction or control. It's important to come up with a plan before you crash and burn.

Operating in crisis mode may seem productive on the surface—being busy can sometimes feel like being important—but it is a dangerous illusion. As Stephen Covey said in *The 7 Habits of Highly Effective People*, "The key is not to prioritize what's on your schedule, but to schedule your priorities." Crisis mode robs you of the clarity needed to define and act on your true priorities.

> **Operating in crisis mode may seem productive on the surface—being busy can sometimes feel like being important—but it is a dangerous illusion.**

Living in a constant state of urgency has real consequences:

- **Physically,** your body stays locked in a stress response, wearing down your immune system, contributing to chronic illnesses, and draining your energy reserves.
- **Emotionally,** you become reactive rather than proactive, allowing external demands to dictate your mood, your choices, and your sense of peace.

- **Relationally,** your ability to connect meaningfully with others diminishes as you operate from a place of survival rather than presence.

- **Spiritually,** crisis mode disconnects you from your deeper sense of purpose, making it harder to hear the quiet but powerful voice guiding your true path.

One of the hidden dangers of living in crisis mode is that over time, we begin to confuse movement with progress. Just because you are busy doesn't mean you are moving forward. In fact, busyness can become a sophisticated form of avoidance, keeping you too distracted to address the deeper shifts that are needed in your life.

> **"Change is inevitable. Growth is optional."**
> **-John C. Maxwell**

Leadership expert John C. Maxwell once said, "Change is inevitable. Growth is optional." Crisis mode forces change upon us, but it rarely leads to growth unless we intentionally choose to step out of the chaos and address the roots of our busyness.

It takes courage to step back and ask hard questions:

- What am I chasing, and why?

- Who or what is determining the pace of my life?

- Is the life I'm busy building actually aligned with my true desires and calling?

Freedom from crisis-mode begins when we acknowledge its cost—and decide we are no longer willing to pay it. As long as we stay trapped in reactivity, we will keep sacrificing our health, peace, relationships, and dreams on the altar of "getting through the day."

You deserve more than survival. You deserve to thrive. And it begins with recognizing that living in constant crisis is not a badge of honor—it's a warning sign. Your life is too precious to spend it putting out fires you were never meant to fight.

Choosing to shift out of crisis mode is not about perfection; it's about progress. It's about choosing to believe that sustainable peace, intentional living, and true purpose are worth fighting for—worth slowing down for—worth reimagining your entire approach to life for.

It's not easy. But neither is living a life where exhaustion and overwhelm are your default settings.

Today, you get to choose a different story.

The Hidden Costs of Crisis Mode

Living in constant crisis mode affects every aspect of our well-being—physically, mentally, emotionally, and even spiritually. Let's consider the following five hidden costs:

1. Physical Exhaustion

Chronic stress weakens the immune system, leads to poor sleep, and increases the risk of conditions like hypertension, diabetes, strokes and heart disease. When your body is always in "fight-or-flight" mode, it never has a chance to rest and recover.

But the wear and tear of physical exhaustion isn't just internal—it's visible. You may notice more frequent colds, slower recovery times, chronic headaches, or weight fluctuations. For women especially, hormone imbalances often result from prolonged stress, contributing to fatigue, brain fog, and emotional instability.

> **When your body is always in "fight-or-flight" mode, it never has a chance to rest and recover.**

The consequences go beyond your health—they affect your ability to show up in your purpose. When your body is in survival mode, dreaming, creating, and thriving are off the table. Rest isn't laziness—it's a strategy for longevity, clarity, and joy. As author and physician Saundra Dalton-Smith writes in *Sacred Rest*, "Sleep is not the same as rest. You can sleep and still wake up exhausted. You need the right kind of rest for restoration."

Reflection Questions:

- How does your body signal that it's overworked or ignored?
- What would true rest look like for you this week?

Write your reflections here:

_____

_____

_____

_____

2. Mental & Emotional Burnout

Crisis mode keeps you stuck in a loop of overwhelm and frustration. It leads to anxiety, brain fog, and an inability to focus or make clear decisions. You may find yourself constantly worrying, second-guessing, or feeling like you're just barely keeping things together.

Over time, burnout begins to warp your self-image. You may begin to question your worth, doubt your capabilities, or feel

> **Crisis mode keeps you stuck in a loop of overwhelm and frustration.**

Intentional Shift: From Crisis to Control

emotionally numb. Decision fatigue becomes real—simple choices feel overwhelming, and important ones get avoided altogether. Burnout also leads to emotional reactivity: the smallest inconvenience can trigger frustration, tears, or shutdown.

Research by the World Health Organization classifies burnout as an occupational phenomenon, but we know it bleeds into personal and spiritual life, too. Without time to regulate emotions, we find ourselves spiraling inward, believing we are failing when we're simply depleted.

One way out of emotional burnout is through emotional hygiene: naming your feelings, practicing self-compassion, and setting clear limits. As psychologist Kristin Neff says, "Self-compassion is not self-indulgence. It is a way to strengthen yourself in times of stress."

Reflection Questions:

- What thoughts repeat themselves when you're mentally overwhelmed?
- When was the last time you felt emotionally steady and centered?

Write your reflections here:

3. Strained Relationships

When you're constantly overwhelmed, it's difficult to show up for yourself, so you will find it just as challenging in your relationships. It can also make it harder to be present and engaged with family, friends, and colleagues.

What we don't process internally, we project externally. Crisis mode can lead us to withdraw, avoid vulnerability, or lash out at those who love us most. We may begin to resent others for their needs or feel unseen in our own.

Healthy relationships require emotional presence. But when we're overwhelmed, we might listen without hearing, show up without truly engaging, or apologize without real repair. Over time, the emotional disconnect creates a wall that love can't penetrate.

> "Most people do not listen with the intent to understand; they listen with the intent to reply."
> -Stephen Covey

As author Stephen Covey reminds us, "Most people do not listen with the intent to understand; they listen with the intent to reply." Crisis mode teaches us to move fast—but relationships require us to slow down.

Reflection Questions:

- Are you emotionally available to those closest to you?
- What relationships have suffered because of your overwhelm?
- Who makes you feel safe, seen, and supported?

Write your reflections here:

_____

_____

_____

_____

4. Loss of Identity & Purpose

When your life revolves around putting out fires, you rarely have time to reflect on who you are and what you truly want.

Living in crisis often reduces you to roles and responsibilities—caregiver, worker, fixer. Over time, you lose sight of who you were before the busyness. Purpose becomes blurry. You wonder what lights you up, what you even enjoy anymore. You may begin to feel disconnected from your passions, goals, and dreams.

> **Rediscovering identity means tuning in to the still, small voice within.**

Rediscovering identity means tuning in to the still, small voice within. It means giving yourself permission to dream again. When you stop striving and start listening, your soul begins to whisper truths: You are more than what you do. You are more than what you carry.

As author Parker Palmer wrote, "Vocation does not come from willfulness. It comes from listening." Crisis shouts, but clarity whispers—and we must create space to hear it.

Reflection Questions:

- What parts of yourself have been buried beneath busyness?
- If you weren't living in reaction mode, what would you pursue?
- What brings you a sense of deep fulfillment?

Write your reflections here:

_____

_____

_____

_____

5. Financial Stress

Living in a reactive state can also impact your financial health. Whether it's impulsive spending due to stress, lack of planning, or an inability to focus on long-term financial stability. Crisis mode can keep you stuck in unhealthy financial patterns.

When finances are out of control, stress rises—and when stress rises, we're more likely to spend emotionally. Crisis mode turns money management into damage control. You delay bills, avoid opening emails, or overextend yourself trying to "keep up."

> **"You must gain control over your money, or the lack of it will forever control you."**
> -Suze Orman

This pattern not only causes anxiety—it creates shame. You may feel like you're failing, even when you're simply overwhelmed and under-supported. But money, like anything else, is a relationship. And relationships require attention, communication, and intentional care.

The shift from scarcity to stewardship begins with small steps: tracking expenses, creating a peace-focused budget, and redefining wealth as freedom—not fear. As Suze Orman says, "You must gain control over your money, or the lack of it will forever control you."

Reflection Questions:

- Are your financial habits driven by peace or pressure?

- What small financial decision can you make this week to regain control?
- Where can you invite help or accountability into your financial life?

Write your reflections here:

_____

_____

_____

_____

Each of these hidden costs compounds the others, making crisis mode feel inescapable. But naming them is the first step to reclaiming your peace, power, and purpose.

Signs You May Be in Crisis Mode

- You wake up feeling tired, no matter how much you sleep.
- You constantly feel overwhelmed and out of control.
- Your health and well-being take a backseat to everything else.

- You find yourself frequently snapping at or withdrawing from loved ones.
- You say "yes" to things even when you want to say "no."
- You feel like life is happening *to* you rather than *for* you.
- You feel like you're "just getting by" instead of truly living.

It's imperative that you be attentive to your full being (mind, body and spirit). We are oftentimes given signals; however, because we never stop, the signal goes unnoticed until it is too late.

If any of these resonate with you, know this—you are not alone, and you *can* shift your story.

The Cost vs. The Choice

Recognizing crisis mode is the first step, but awareness without action won't create change. Staying in this cycle is high, but the good news is that you have a choice.

Living in crisis mode demands a price too high to pay. You will pay on the front end or the back end—but you will pay. So why not make the choice to do it differently?

> **Living in crisis mode demands a price too high to pay.**

I had to make that choice. It wasn't easy. I had built a life of performance and perfection, running from one responsibility to another while my health quietly deteriorated. I wore busyness like a badge of honor. But when my body shut down and forced me to face my truth, I had to choose -- stay stuck in the familiar discomfort of crisis mode or do the hard work of shifting toward intentional control.

The shift demanded change—physically, emotionally, and spiritually. It required me to set boundaries, say no more often, and reevaluate how I defined success. But what I gained was far greater than what I gave up. I found peace. I found purpose. I found the version of me I had buried beneath years of doing instead of being.

> **Comfort zones feel safe, but they are not always sacred.**

Comfort zones feel safe, but they are not always sacred. If you're not careful, comfort will become your cage. It's not about blaming yourself for the season you've been in, it's about **empowering yourself to shift forward.**

You have the power to move from exhaustion to empowerment, from chaos to clarity, from being pulled by life to leading your life. The choice is yours.

Ask yourself:

- What is it really costing me to stay the same?
- What might I gain if I choose differently?

- What shift is my soul asking me to make today?

Change begins with a choice. Make yours today.

In the next section, we'll explore how you can start making that shift today. Are you ready?

ROBYN T. JONES

THE SHIFT FROM CRISIS TO CONTROL

Making the shift from crisis mode to control doesn't happen overnight, but it starts with a decision—the decision to take back ownership of your life. When I finally realized that I was stuck in a cycle of stress and survival, I had to make a conscious choice to shift. That choice led to a series of small but powerful changes that transformed the way I live, work, and engage with the world.

But let's be honest, deciding to shift is not always celebrated by others. When you start setting new boundaries, prioritizing rest, or saying no to things that once consumed you, it may confuse or even disappoint people who benefited from your crisis mode. That's why I always say: the decision to shift is **for YOU**, not for them.

> **When you start setting new boundaries, prioritizing rest, or saying no to things that once consumed you, it may confuse or even disappoint people who benefited from your crisis mode.**

Shifting requires courage. It means stepping away from familiar dysfunction and toward a future that feels uncertain—but full of possibility. It means taking responsibility for your peace, your pace, and your priorities, even when it's uncomfortable.

When I began my journey, I had to grieve the version of me that stayed busy just to feel useful. I had to unlearn patterns that were praised—like overworking, overcommitting, and overlooking my needs. But on the other side of that discomfort was clarity, control, and confidence.

> **You can't fix what you don't acknowledge.**

There are steps that will help you in your journey, which I call the *four A's* of shifting: Awareness, Acceptance, Alignment, and Action. These are not just concepts—they are building blocks. Each one brings you closer to a life that isn't built around surviving but thriving. Let's take them one step at a time:

Intentional Shifting: Four 'A' Steps

Step 1: Awareness – Recognizing the Patterns

Awareness is where every meaningful transformation begins. It's the light that reveals the path forward, the lens that helps you see your life clearly—not just how it looks on the outside, but how it feels on the inside. You can't change what you refuse to confront, and you can't fix what you don't first acknowledge.

Living in crisis mode for so long can create blind spots. You might normalize the stress, the exhaustion, or the constant rushing. It can become so familiar that you forget there's another way to live. Awareness disrupts that narrative. It says, "Pause. Look. Reflect."

Intentional Shift: From Crisis to Control

When I began my own journey, I had to face some difficult truths. I had to admit that I wasn't just tired, I was depleted. I wasn't just busy—I was burying myself in tasks to avoid stillness. I wasn't just managing responsibilities, I was ignoring warning signs from my body, my relationships, and my spirit. It was sobering. But it was also the beginning of something beautiful: clarity.

Awareness doesn't come with shame—it comes with insight. It invites you to explore where things are off track, not to condemn yourself, but to create space for compassion and change. This is not about blaming yourself for where you are. It's about owning your journey and being honest about what's no longer serving you.

> **Awareness doesn't come with shame—it comes with insight.**

Start small. Pay attention to what drains you and what restores you. Notice your habits, your patterns, and your self-talk. What do you tolerate that deep down you know you shouldn't? What do you avoid because it's easier not to deal with it?

Awareness is powerful—but only if you act on it. In the next steps, you'll begin learning how to shift, but for now, take the time to truly see your life without filters or excuses. You are not powerless. You are paying attention—and that changes everything.

Questions to Ponder:

- In what areas of your life do you feel out of control?
- What recurring stressors keep you in crisis mode?
- How does crisis mode affect your emotions, decisions, and well-being?

Step 2: Acceptance – Owning Your Power

Acceptance doesn't mean you have to like where you are; it means owning your power to change it. It's easy to resist acceptance because it often feels like surrender, like giving up. But true acceptance is not passive—it's powerful. It's the courageous decision to face your reality without denial, without blame, and without shame.

When I reached the point where my life demanded change, I had to accept that my pace, my patterns, and even my perceptions were no longer serving me. It was humbling to admit that I wasn't as in control as I thought. Yet it was also freeing. Acceptance opened the door to action.

> **Acceptance acknowledges what *is* so that you can create what *can be*.**

Acceptance acknowledges what *is* so that you can create what *can be*. It shifts your energy from frustration to focus. Instead of pouring energy into resisting your circumstances, you can start pouring energy into rewriting your story.

Acceptance doesn't mean settling—it means choosing. Choosing to see your power even in difficult seasons. Choosing to believe that new outcomes are possible. Choosing to show up for yourself, even if no one else fully understands your journey.

Mantras to Ground Your Acceptance:

- *I am in control of my life. I have the power to change my circumstances.*
- *I release what no longer serves me and embrace what strengthens me.*
- *I honor my journey, knowing that acceptance is the first step toward transformation.*

Acceptance clears the fog and lays the foundation for intentional living. It's where the real work—and the real healing—begins.

Step 3: Alignment – Setting Your Intentions

Once you recognize and accept where you are, it's time to align your life with where you want to be. Alignment is the bridge between insight and action. It requires intentional reflection and courageous decision-making. Without alignment, your life will continue to feel disjointed—like your heart is going one direction while your habits are pulling another.

Alignment isn't about perfection—it's about integration. It's the process of bringing your thoughts, behaviors, and daily routines into harmony with the life you want to create. This means getting honest about what no longer fits, what needs to be added, and what must be released.

During my own journey, alignment required me to make difficult but necessary shifts. I had to ask: Am I living in a way that honors my values? Are my calendar and commitments aligned with what truly matters to me? This step isn't just about what you say you value—it's about what your actions confirm.

Sometimes, alignment will ask you to slow down. Sometimes, it will ask you to say no. And almost always, it will ask you to listen—really listen—to what your soul is craving beneath the noise.

The beautiful thing about alignment is that it brings peace. Even if life still has challenges, you'll feel more grounded, more authentic, and more energized because you're no longer living in conflict with yourself.

> **Sometimes, alignment will ask you to slow down. Sometimes, it will ask you to say no. And almost always, it will ask you to listen— really listen—to what your soul is craving beneath the noise.**

Ask yourself:

- What do I truly want for my life?
- What values do I want to prioritize?

- What small, consistent changes can I make to move toward my desired life?

Step 4: Action – Implementing Change Daily

Shifting from crisis to control is about taking consistent, intentional action. The key is to start small so the changes feel manageable. Often, we get overwhelmed by the idea of transformation because we imagine it has to be grand or immediate. But in truth, sustainable change happens in the small, quiet choices we make every single day.

> **But in truth, sustainable change happens in the small, quiet choices we make every single day.**

Intentional living requires follow-through. It's not enough to know where you're going—you have to take steps in that direction. Progress may be slow at first, but each small win builds momentum. It's not about perfection; it's about persistence.

Here are a few practical ways to begin:

1. **Start Your Day with a Grounding Ritual**
   Instead of jumping into chaos, create a morning routine that centers you. This could include journaling, prayer, meditation, stretching, or even sitting in silence for five

minutes. Starting your day with calm intention sets the tone for everything that follows. It reminds your mind and body that you are in control.

✦ ***Mini Reflection:*** What simple ritual can I add tomorrow morning that brings me peace?

Write your reflections here:

_____

_____

_____

_____

2. Prioritize Rest & Recovery

Sleep, self-care, and setting boundaries are non-negotiable. Rest is not just about sleep—it's about restoration. Whether it's saying no to a commitment, taking a 15-minute walk, or unplugging from screens, rest allows you to recover and realign with what matters.

✦ ***Mini Reflection:*** What does rest look like for me today and how can I honor it?

Intentional Shift: From Crisis to Control

Write your reflections here:

_____

_____

_____

_____

3. Plan with Purpose

Use a planner or digital calendar to structure your day. Don't just schedule appointments—schedule space for yourself. Structure gives your day direction and reduces decision fatigue. You'll be amazed at how ten minutes of focused planning each morning can shift your whole day.

✨ ***Mini Reflection:*** What's one small thing I can plan today that supports my values?

Write your reflections here:

_____

_____

_____

_____

4. Practice Saying No

Every yes is a no to something else. When you say no to what drains you, you make room for what fuels you. Practice setting loving, firm boundaries—not as rejection, but as protection of your peace.

✨ *Mini Reflection:* What do I need to say "no" to today to say "yes" to myself?

Write your reflections here:

_____

_____

_____

_____

5. Surround Yourself with Support

Growth is hard to sustain in isolation. Find your tribe—those who support your shift, remind you of your strength, and speak life into your journey. Whether it's a friend, a coach, or a community group, surround yourself with voices that echo your intentions.

Intentional Shift: From Crisis to Control

✦ *Mini Reflection:* Who helps me feel supported, grounded, and seen?

Write your reflections here:

_____

_____

_____

_____

Each step you take reinforces your decision to shift from crisis to control. Action breathes life into your awareness, acceptance, and alignment. It's the final piece of the puzzle—and the one that will carry you forward.

The shift from crisis to control is not about perfection — it's about progress. Every small step you take adds up, creating momentum that leads to lasting transformation.

Imagine your life six months from now: waking up feeling empowered and in control, making intentional choices that align with your values, and experiencing a sense of peace and fulfillment. That future is possible, and it starts with the choices you make today and recognizing who's in your corner.

> **The shift from crisis to control is not about perfection—it's about progress.**

Are you ready to anchor down and keep going forward? Let's move forward together!

LIFE ANCHORS:
FAITH, FAMILY, and FRIENDS

When life feels overwhelming, it's easy to feel isolated. When operating in crisis mode, we often turn inward instead of outward. It grieves my spirit when I hear others say they don't need anyone, or they can do it alone. We've all heard the expression, "No man is an island." But it's more than a phrase, it's a spiritual and emotional truth. We were never meant to navigate life alone.

> **We were never meant to navigate life alone.**

In fact, during some of my most difficult seasons—moments when I was exhausted, discouraged, or unsure—I was reminded of the power of people. Not just crowds or acquaintances, but real connections. The ones that call you out and call you up. The ones that show up without being asked. The ones who see you not only as you are, but who you're becoming.

When you're making a shift from crisis to control, these life anchors become even more essential. Why? Because change, even good change, is uncomfortable. Letting go of patterns that kept you busy but burned out is not always easy. It can be lonely. And that's where your anchors come in.

There are three anchors that have helped me navigate a life filled with uncertainty, particularly regarding my health. I've learned to keep them nourished, because when storms come—and they will—it's those anchors that keep you from drifting away from yourself. They remind you of who you are, whose you are, and what matters most.

These anchors are **Faith, Family, and Friends.** They each offer something unique. Faith connects us to our source and gives us strength beyond ourselves. Family keeps us grounded in love, truth, and accountability. Friends walk with us, not because they have to, but because they choose to.

When these areas are thriving, they don't just support you—they lift you. They empower your shift. They reinforce the idea that intentional living isn't a solo journey. It's a supported one.

Let's take a deeper look at these three life anchors and reflect on how you can strengthen each one for your own journey.

Faith: The Foundation of Strength

"Faith is taking the first step even when you don't see the whole staircase."
— Dr. Martin Luther King Jr.

Faith is more than a belief system—it is a lifeline.

Faith provides a deep sense of hope and resilience, especially in difficult seasons. It reminds us that we are not alone and that there is a greater plan for our lives. Whether through prayer, meditation, scripture, or personal reflection, faith gives us the peace we need to move forward with confidence.

But faith is more than a belief system—it is a lifeline. In the midst of crisis, when logic fails and strength feels scarce, faith becomes the place we go to lay down our burdens and pick up courage. It becomes the whisper that says, "You will make it through," when everything around you say otherwise.

There were moments in my own journey when faith was all I had. When answers were few and the weight of responsibility threatened to break me, I turned inward—and upward. It was in those moments of stillness and surrender that I found clarity. Faith reminded me that I didn't have to have it all together to be held together. I didn't have to know the next step to keep going.

Scripture says in Hebrews 11:1, *"Now faith is the substance of things hoped for, the evidence of things not seen."* Faith is choosing to believe there is more—even when we can't see it yet. It's trusting that the process has purpose, that the storm will pass, and that your steps are being ordered even when the path looks uncertain.

Faith invites us to slow down. It shifts our gaze from what's happening *to* us to what God may be doing *in* us. It strengthens us not just to endure—but to grow. To deepen. To emerge from the storm more grounded, more focused, and more connected to our source.

You may express your faith through traditional practices or quiet moments of reflection. You may sing, write in a journal, walk in nature, or read sacred texts. However, you connect with the divine, know that it's okay to bring your questions, your weariness, and your hope to the altar. Faith can carry what you cannot.

Ask yourself:

- How does my faith sustain me in challenging moments?
- What practices strengthen my spiritual connection?
- How can I lean into my faith when life feels out of control?

Family: The Mirror of Love and Accountability

"Family is not an important thing, it's everything."
— Michael J. Fox

Family, whether chosen or biological, is often our greatest support system. They remind us of who we are when we forget. They ground us in truth when we drift. And they hold up a mirror—not just reflecting our love, but sometimes revealing our growth edges.

Intentional Shift: From Crisis to Control

During my own shift from crisis to control, it was my family who walked beside me, even when they didn't always understand what I was doing or why I needed to change. Their patience taught me grace. Their honesty taught me strength. Their presence reminded me that healing isn't just an individual process—it's communal. And yet, family dynamics can be complex. Love doesn't always come in the form we expect or want. That's why intention is key.

> **Healthy family relationships don't just happen; they're cultivated.**

Healthy family relationships don't just happen; they're cultivated. They require time, vulnerability, boundaries, and forgiveness. They require us to show up consistently, to listen actively, and to communicate openly. And sometimes, they require distance or healing space in order for growth to occur.

> **The truth is, not every family relationship will be a source of comfort.**

The truth is, not every family relationship will be a source of comfort. Some may be strained, broken, or emotionally exhausting. And part of shifting into intentional living is discerning which connections need nurturing, which need boundaries, and which need release.

Still, when family is aligned with love and accountability, it becomes a powerful anchor. It keeps us from drifting too far. It reminds us of our roots. And it reflects the kind of support we often don't know we need until we feel it.

Whether it's a parent, a sibling, a cousin, or a close friend who feels like family—invest in those bonds. Express gratitude. Initiate healing conversations. Be the first to forgive. Create space for honesty and growth. Family is not perfect, but it can be sacred.

> **Family is not perfect, but it can be sacred.**

Consider:

- Who in my family provides encouragement and wisdom?
- How can I be more intentional in nurturing these relationships?
- Are there any family dynamics that need healing or attention?

Friends: The Power of Community and Encouragement

"A friend is someone who knows the song in your heart and can sing it back to you when you have forgotten the words."
— C.S. Lewis

True friendships bring joy, perspective, and encouragement. Friends can help us navigate life's ups and downs, celebrate our wins, and provide wisdom in tough times. But friendships—like any meaningful connection—require intention and care.

During my personal shift from crisis to control, I began to evaluate who had truly been there during my lowest moments—not just the ones who celebrated my success, but those who checked in when my light dimmed. I realized that real friends don't just agree with you. They challenge you. They love you enough to hold a mirror up and say, "You're better than this," when you're slipping, and "I see you," when you feel invisible.

Intentional friendships are not about quantity, but quality. Having a small circle of friends who understand your journey, respect your boundaries, and root for your growth is far more valuable than being surrounded by people who only show up when it's convenient.

And as much as friendships can nourish, they can also require boundaries. Not every friend is meant to walk with you into your next season. Some may drain your energy, pull you back into crisis patterns, or resist the changes you're making. That's okay. As you shift, your relationships will shift too.

The key is discernment: who adds to your peace? Who challenges your thinking in love? Who supports your evolution, not just your image? These are the friends who help anchor you when life feels unsteady.

Be that kind of friend too. Reach out first. Offer grace. Speak truth in love. Create space for real conversation, not just surface updates. Friendship is a gift—and like any gift, it grows in value the more it's nurtured.

Reflect on:

- Do my friendships add value and positivity to my life?
- How can I be a better friend to those who support me?
- Are there friendships I need to nurture or set boundaries around?

Nurturing Your Anchors for a Balanced Life

Anchors are not just meant to exist, they are meant to be maintained, strengthened, and protected. Like a tree that flourishes when nourished, your life anchors grow stronger the more you invest in them. The more you care for something, the stronger it grows. What you nurture, you strengthen. Your anchors are living connections that require intentional care, not occasional attention.

> **Your anchors are living connections that require intentional care, not occasional attention.**

To stay grounded and supported through life's shifts, here are four ways you can nurture these vital relationships:

1. Set Aside Time for Spiritual Growth

Faith is like a muscle—the more you exercise it, the stronger it becomes. Carve out intentional time each day or week to connect with something higher than yourself. Read sacred texts, pray, meditate, journal your prayers, or join faith-based communities. Feed your soul the same way you feed your body—regularly and intentionally.

✨ ***Mini Challenge:*** Choose one small spiritual habit to practice for the next 7 days.

2. Schedule Regular Family Check-ins

Family bonds can easily fray when left unattended. It doesn't always have to be grand gestures, simple, consistent communication matters. Call a loved one just to say hello. Send a text to check in, even when life is busy.
The pandemic taught us an important lesson: connection cannot be postponed. Prioritize those you love while you have the opportunity.

✨ *Mini Challenge:* Schedule one meaningful family check-in this week (even a short one).

3. Be Present in Friendships

Friendships thrive on shared moments, not just shared history. When spending time with friends, practice putting away your phone or other distractions. Truly listen. Laugh together. Cry together. Celebrate wins and mourn losses side by side. Presence is the greatest gift you can offer.

✨ *Mini Challenge:* Plan one distraction-free moment or outing with a friend you cherish.

4. Express Gratitude Intentionally

Gratitude strengthens the heart of every relationship. Don't wait for big occasions—make gratitude a daily practice. Write a note, send a heartfelt text, or simply tell someone how much they mean to you. Gratitude multiplies connection and deepens trust.

✨ *Mini Challenge:* Express genuine gratitude to three people this week.

When you nurture your anchors, you don't just survive life's storms, you grow through them. You build a life where you are supported, seen, and strengthened at every step of your journey from crisis to control.

Remember, just as you commit to nurturing others, it's equally important to communicate what *you* need from them. Healthy relationships are not built on assumption; they are built on open dialogue and mutual growth.

Reflection Question:
Who are your anchors—and how will you intentionally strengthen those connections today?

Write your reflections here:

_____

_____

_____

_____

_____

ANCHORING YOUR SHIFT: REFLECTIONS & JOURNALING

Anchoring your shift begins with deep reflection. Taking time to pause, process, and put your thoughts on paper is a powerful way to move from surviving to thriving. Writing slows you down, sharpens your awareness, and helps you see patterns and possibilities you may otherwise miss. Journaling creates space for growth—first on the page, and then in your life.

As Anne Lamott wisely said, *"Almost everything will work again if you unplug it for a few minutes, including you."* Journaling is that moment of unplugging. It's the sacred space where you recalibrate, refocus, and realign with your true self. When life pulls you into chaos, journaling gently pulls you back into clarity.

In the silence of journaling, we often hear the loudest truths of our hearts. Be intentional in sitting silently with yourself.

Reflection is not about rushing to solve everything— it's about learning to sit with what is, so you can build from a place of honesty and intention.

> **Reflection is not about rushing to solve everything—it's about learning to sit with what is, so you can build from a place of honesty and intention.**

These prompts are designed to help you explore your thoughts, emotions, and experiences so you can strengthen the foundation of your shift. They are not about perfection—they are about connection. Connecting to yourself, your purpose, and your deepest desires.

Take your time. Come back to these questions often. They are anchors you can return to anytime you feel the pull of old habits or the weight of uncertainty. Let them ground you in who you are becoming.

Self-Discovery Reflections

- Describe a recent moment where you felt completely overwhelmed. What caused it, and how did you respond?

- Think about a time when you felt truly at peace. What were the circumstances that allowed you to feel that way?

Intentional Shift: From Crisis to Control

- What limiting beliefs or fears keep you stuck in crisis mode? How can you begin to challenge them?

- If you had all the time and energy you needed, what would you want to create or accomplish in your life?

Faith, Family, and Friends Journaling Prompts

- How has your faith sustained you during difficult times? Reflect on a moment when your faith provided clarity or peace.

- Write about a time when a family member or close friend showed up for you in a meaningful way. How did it impact you?

- How can you be more intentional about nurturing your relationships with the people who matter most?

Practical Journaling Prompts for Taking Action

- Identify three small changes you can make this week to regain control over your life.

- Write a letter to your future self, describing how your life has changed after making the shift from crisis to control.

- Make a list of boundaries you need to establish in your life to protect your peace and well-being.

- What are three affirmations you can start saying daily to reinforce your commitment to intentional living?

Intentional Shift: From Crisis to Control

_____

_____

_____

_____

By reflecting on these prompts regularly, you'll deepen your awareness, strengthen your mindset, and stay aligned with your journey toward a life of purpose and peace.

"Self-reflection is the school of wisdom."
— *Baltasar Gracián*

Remember: Your growth is not measured by how fast you move, but by your willingness to keep showing up for yourself— one honest reflection at a time.

ROBYN T. JONES

Intentional Shift: From Crisis to Control

THE LIFT & SHIFT™ CHALLENGE

When the words *Lift & Shift™* first dropped into my spirit, I knew they carried the heart of my work. I built my speaking, coaching, and training business around helping women transition from reactive, crisis-based living to intentional, controlled, purpose-driven lives.

Now, it's your turn.

To truly experience the shift from crisis to control, you must take consistent, intentional action. That's why I've created a simple **4-week Lift & Shift™ challenge** for you, based on the Four A's you explored earlier in the book.

Each week focuses on one principle, with simple steps to implement. These are not meant to overwhelm you, they are designed to empower you to shift steadily, one week at a time.

Week 1: Awareness – Identifying the Areas of Crisis

- Reflect on where you feel most out of control (health, finances, relationships, etc.).
- Identify the emotional and physical effects of living in crisis mode.
- Begin tracking stressors and triggers throughout your day.

✨ *Action Step:* Keep a Crisis to Clarity Journal, noting moments of overwhelm and what triggered them.

Week 2: Acceptance – Embracing Where You Are

- Acknowledge that change starts with honesty.
- Release guilt or shame tied to past decisions.
- Offer yourself grace as you move toward transformation.

✨ *Action Step:* Write a Letter of Release, forgiving yourself and committing to a new path forward.

Week 3: Alignment – Shaping a New Mindset

- Set clear, intentional goals that align with your true values.
- Establish small, sustainable habits to support your vision.
- Reframe negative self-talk with empowering affirmations.

✨ *Action Step:* Create a Daily Intention Statement to anchor your mindset each morning.

Week 4: Action – Implementing Real Change

- Prioritize activities that bring peace and fulfillment.

- Strengthen boundaries that protect your energy.
- Stay consistent with new habits to build momentum.

✦ ***Action Step:*** Develop a Lift & Shift Action Plan with three non-negotiable habits to maintain balance and control.

Embracing the Shift

By following these *Lift & Shift*™ principles in action, you're not just making temporary adjustments, you're creating a lifestyle of purposeful intentionality.

Every small step you take moves you closer to a life where you lead instead of react; thrive instead of survive; and live fully instead of merely existing.

The shift starts with a single decision. Choose yourself today. Choose your life.

ROBYN T. JONES

THE SHIFT STARTS NOW

Right now, in this very moment, you are standing at a crossroads—the choice to continue in crisis mode or to shift into a life of clarity, control, and purpose. The decision is yours. The power has always been in your hands.

Imagine waking up each day feeling anchored, intentional, and in control of your emotions, your time, and your energy. Picture yourself moving through life with focus and peace, no longer reacting to the chaos around you but shaping your path with purpose and power.

This shift is not just about breaking free from crisis mode—it's about creating a life that reflects who you truly are. It's about choosing health over burnout, peace over pressure, and fulfillment over frustration.

But here's the truth: the shift won't happen by accident. It requires a conscious decision, an inner commitment to no longer live on autopilot. It demands courage to change the narrative you've been telling yourself—the one that says you must accept exhaustion, overwhelm, and survival as your norm.

The shift begins with self-awareness—recognizing where you are, why you are there, and where you truly desire to be.

there, and where you truly desire to be. It continues with acceptance—owning your journey without shame or regret. It solidifies through alignment—choosing to align your actions with your values and your vision. And it flourishes through action—taking consistent, intentional steps toward the life you desire and deserve.

You are not powerless. You are not stuck. You are not too late.

Every new day, every new breath, offers you a fresh opportunity to choose differently. And it is in these small, sacred choices that transformation begins.

When you choose to shift, you give yourself permission to:

- Set healthier boundaries that honor your peace and protect your energy.
- Prioritize your well-being without guilt or apology.
- Pursue passions and dreams that have been waiting patiently for you to say yes.
- Deepen your relationships by showing up more present, more authentic, and more alive.

The journey won't always be easy. Old habits will beckon you back to the familiar comfort of chaos. Fear will whisper that change is too hard. Doubt will try to convince you that you are not capable of more.

But remember this: you are capable. You are worthy. And you are equipped with everything you need to shift into a life of clarity, control, and purpose.

Intentional Shift: From Crisis to Control

Your shift begins now.

I challenge you to make this commitment: No more waiting. No more delaying your own peace, your own happiness, or your own healing. No more telling yourself that "one day" you'll live the life you envision.

Today is your "one day." Today, you take your power back. Today, you choose to lead your life with intention, strength, and hope.

Let this moment mark the beginning of your intentional shift. Stop and make a conscious decision that surviving is no longer enough. Let this be the day you choose to live fully, boldly, and unapologetically.

The world is waiting for the fullness of who you are.

Reflect and Take Action:

- **What's one small step you can take today that moves you closer to the life you want?**
  Write it down and commit to it.

- **Who can support you on this journey?**
  Reach out to them and share your commitment to intentional living.

- **How will you remind yourself daily that you are shifting from crisis to control?**
  Create a personal affirmation and speak it over your life every day.

> "The smallest step in the right direction can turn out to be the biggest step of your life."
> — *Unknown*

RECOMMENDED READING

As you continue your journey towards an intentional shift, I encourage you to explore additional transformational resources that inspire growth, healing, and empowerment. Here are a few books that have deeply impacted my own shift and may inspire you as well:

- *The Power of Now* by Eckhart Tolle
- *Atomic Habits* by James Clear
- *Boundaries* by Dr. Henry Cloud & Dr. John Townsend
- *Radical Awakening* by Dr. Shefali Tsabary
- *The Gifts of Imperfection* by Brené Brown
- *Purpose Driven Life* by Rick Warren
- *The 15 Invaluable Laws of Growth* by John C. Maxwell
- *What To Do Next: Taking Your Best Steps When Life Is Uncertain* by Jeff Henderson
- *Find Your Why* by Simon Sinek

Reading widely and intentionally can help reinforce the powerful shift you're making—from living in crisis to living in control.

ROBYN T. JONES

NEXT STEPS FOR YOUR INTENTIONAL SHIFT

Congratulations on taking the first steps toward living intentionally and reclaiming your life from crisis mode.

Your journey doesn't have to end here.

If you're ready for deeper tools, personalized coaching, or additional *Lift & Shift*™ resources designed to support your growth, I invite you to connect with me.

My journey reshaped me from the inside out and gave me a more passionate and determined heart to serve other women who are ready to live intentionally. Together, we can build a life anchored in clarity, control, and purpose.

✨ **Scan the QR code below to connect for personal or group coaching, keynote speaking, and leadership training services. Discover how you can shift boldly into your next season of intentional living!**

ROBYN T. JONES

ACKNOWLEDGEMENTS

To my husband, Contrell Jones—thank you for your unwavering support, patience, and love throughout this journey. Your encouragement and creativity, especially in bringing my book's cover vision to life, gave me the strength to finish strong. I couldn't have done this without you.

To my family—your love has been a constant foundation, especially during my years of living in crisis. I'm deeply grateful for each of you and appreciate you being pillars to lean on.

To my editor, Dr. Antiwan Walker—thank you for lending your expertise, keen eye, and thoughtful feedback to help bring this vision to life.

To my dearest and closest friends—thank you for your encouragement, wisdom, and persistent nudges to finish what I started. Your love and support carried me through days of frustration and overwhelm.

To my Next Level Coach, Cledra Gross—thank you for helping me embrace who God called me to be and for reminding me of the value of investing in myself.

To Dr. Catrise Austin—thank you for sharing your framework which encouraged and helped me bring this project to life. Your guidance was a true gift.

Thank you all.
This book exists because of your belief in me.

www.ingramcontent.com/pod-product-compliance
Lightning Source LLC
Chambersburg PA
CBHW031210090426
42736CB00009B/856

OTHER
/
WISE

Gregory Dunne

ISOBAR
PRESS

First published in 2019 by

Isobar Press
Sakura 2-21-23-202, Setagaya-ku,
Tokyo 156-0053, Japan
&
14 Isokon Flats, Lawn Road,
London NW3 2XD, United Kingdom

https://isobarpress.com

ISBN 978-4-907359-27-0

Copyright © Gregory Dunne, 2019
All rights reserved.

ACKNOWLEDGEMENTS

Grateful acknowledgement is made to the editors of the journals in which some of these poems, or versions of them, first appeared: *Cha: An Asian Literary Magazine, cold drill, Crazyhorse, Hummingbird, Kyoto Journal, Mainichi Daily News, Modern Haiku, Poetry East, Poetry Kanto, Rock and Sling, Verse and Voice, Yomimono*. A number of the poems also appeared in *Fistful of Lotus* (Elizabeth Forrest, 2000) and in *Home Test* (Adastra Press, 2009): many thanks to Elizabeth Forrest and Gary Metras respectively.

Translations of Santōka's poetry are from *Walking into the Wind, A Sweep of Poems by Santōka, Versions by Cid Corman* (Cadmus Editions, 1990). Grateful acknowledgment is made to Bob Arnold, the executor of the Cid Corman estate, for permission to use these translations.

Cover image by Sarah Brayer, *The Red Line*, 2016; back-cover photograph of Gregory Dunne in Cid Corman's CC coffee shop, Kyoto, by Dennis Maloney.